Juicing Recipes For Weight Loss

Lose Weight, Gain Energy And Improve Health with Delicious Juice Recipes

Donna Hardin

Juicing Recipes For Weight Loss

Lose Weight, Gain Energy And Improve Health with Delicious Juice Recipes

Table of Contents

Preface

Hello, and welcome to the wonderful world of juicing!

My name is Donna Hardin and I'm about to take you on a journey which will show you all you need to know about juicing fruits and vegetables – the wonderful benefits, how a juicing diet can help you transform your body and how to properly use fresh juices to cleanse, detox and ultimately lose that extra weight that just doesn't want to come off for some reason.

I have been a believer that fruit and vegetable juices will change your health and your life for the better since Day One. Now, with over a decade of juicing experience and consultation from top nutritionists across the country, I compiled all the knowledge and secrets I accumulated into this book, so you can benefit from it.

I am sure I am not the only woman who has a very busy everyday schedule. But, despite this, I found a simple way to lose weight, feel energized and live a healthier, happier life.

Now I am willing to share the knowledge about juicing that I have accumulated throughout the years with you.

Right here, right now, is your chance to lose weight and improve your overall health. Are you ready for the journey? It's going to be a fun one!

In the first part of the book I cover all the amazing benefits of fresh juices, how your body changes for the better and how exactly can someone lose weight by drinking fruit and vegetable juices.

You can skip this part and jump straight to the recipes if you're in a hurry, but I strongly recommend you read this part first.

Remember that your mind plays an equally if not more important role than what you actually eat or drink. So preparing your mind for what you'll experience in the next few days and weeks is crucial.

Let's get started!

Ready, Set, Juice!

There is an old saying that goes: "You are what you eat." Basically it means that if you eat healthy, you will remain healthy. But if you don't, well, you know how that will turn out.

I cannot stress enough how important it is to consider your food choices. What we choose to eat daily is one of the biggest factors that contributes to our body's state of health.

Our food choices also help us achieve various health goals that we may have – whether it is as simple as getting rid of pimples or as big as losing weight.

And speaking of weight loss, did you know that the most effective way to lose weight is to do it naturally?

While there are a myriad of methods which you can use to naturally lose weight, there is one particular method that I would love to discuss with you and it's called juicing.

Juicing and Blending

You probably have the occasional smoothie at home – you know, using a blender to puree different fruits so that you can have a glass of sweet, nutritious goodness.

Green drinks are mostly associated with blending because most people either don't know what juicing is or

11

they use 'blending' and 'juicing' interchangeably. The fact is, the two methods are entirely different.

To put it simply, juicing is extracting the liquid nutrition out of fresh fruits and vegetables, leaving the pulp behind. Like blending, it is another great way to get vital nutrients from fresh produce into the body – through a green drink.

Both methods provide different health benefits and a great end result when it comes to using raw produce to nourish the body.

Which method is better depends solely on personal preference. The same goes for when you're aiming to lose some weight, as both methods are proven to be effective. People can either undergo a fruit/vegetable juice therapy or include healthy smoothies in their diets for weight loss.

So whether you go for a juice or a smoothie (or both!) what's important is that you make use of nutrient-dense foods (aka fruits and vegetables) to get the most out each method.

I would recommend both methods but personally, I juice more than I blend, so juicing will be our main focus for this book.

How does juicing work?

The main goal of a fruit and vegetable juice therapy is to transfer the fresh produce's vital nutrients (which are dissolved in its juices) into the body, particularly into the blood and lymph streams.

The juice therapy begins as a cleansing process, providing the proper minerals to cleanse the lymph stream.

The lymph stream's main responsibility is to continuously cleanse the body and protect it against harmful chemicals, so if it is polluted with chemical toxins and toxic materials, it won't be able to do its job.

Consuming mineral-rich fruit and vegetable juices packed with bio-organic calcium is the best way to go if you want your lymph stream to be cleansed. Once your lymph stream is toxin-free, it will be able to cleanse the rest of the body, which in turn helps the body absorb the essential nutrients it needs to be able to function properly.

"But what does this have to do with losing weight?" Well, you know how we were always taught how important it is to eat a balanced diet? A balanced diet helps keep our bodies fit, preventing us from being overweight.

A truly balanced diet is 50% cleansing and 50% building. Only when a diet removes harmful toxins from the tissues and at the same time repairs and restores tissue integrity is it rightfully called balanced.

Now, that's exactly what fruit and vegetable juices do – they cleanse and build the body, providing everything you need from a balanced diet.

So go on this journey with me and learn how juicing can help you shed off those extra pounds. Read on and later you will surely be asking yourself "Why have I never tried juicing before?"

Why Do We Need To Juice?

At this point you may be wondering, why do we need to juice our fruits and vegetables when we can readily eat them?

The simple answer would be that it takes several hours to digest solid food, sometimes so long that its nourishment has decreased before finally reaching the body's cells and tissues.

Let's take celery as an example.

Celery is known to fight against the effects of extreme heat because it is packed with sodium chloride. Say you were experiencing very hot weather and decided to eat a lot of celery sticks to counteract the heat's effects. But before you could obtain the vegetable's beneficial effects, your body would have already succumbed to the heat because celery sticks take too long to digest.

That's where the beauty of juicing comes in.

If you juiced your celery instead of simply eating it, your body could have fought against the heat faster than you think. This is because the juice extracted from fresh, organic fruits or vegetables nourishes the body and provides the nutrients it needs in a manner that they can be most readily assimilated and digested.

The Importance of Juicing

The most important benefits of fruit and vegetable juices for our bodies is their ability to balance a diet, and cleanse and build the body, starting with our cells.

Our cells are constantly damaged. To restore damaged cells, we need vital juices that can transmit the energies of the air, water and sun into our bodies. One of the main functions of our blood is to transport all the important energies and nutrients to where they are needed in the body, including our cells.

Because of this, it is safe to assume that blood is the life force in our body. Without healthy blood, not one part of our body would be nourished and would therefore not be able to properly function.

That's why it is important to saturate our blood with as many essential vitamins, nutrients and enzymes as we can – and this can be achieved through consumption of fresh fruit and vegetable juices.

If you're wondering how powerful juice therapy is, you should know that many medical experts believe that fresh fruit and vegetable juices should be used as a supplement to an average person's regular diet.

So basically, what I'm trying to emphasize is that liquefied foods, especially fruit and vegetable juices, are easier to digest compared to solid foods, whether cooked or raw. The soluble nutrients found in fruit and vegetable juices are the easiest to take into the body. It is not about what you eat, what is important is what you absorb. If you don't properly absorb the vitamins and minerals from the food you consume, your body will become weak.

Do you recall that when you were sick as a child, your mom would make you drink a lot of water and feed you only hot soup? This is because when the body has no energy and vitality, it does not assimilate foods well.

Comparatively speaking, the body does not take much value from consumed foods unless they are in liquid form where the nutrients are more easily digested.

So now, even if you're not sick, you know you're not perfectly healthy. You need the power of healthy juices to keep you nourished, to keep you fit.

Yes, that's how important juicing your fruits and vegetables is. That's how much you need to stay healthy.

The Real Benefits of Fruits and Vegetables

In the previous chapter we learned why we need to juice our fruits and vegetables as well as the importance of juicing.

Now we are at the second stop of our journey and in this chapter we will be learning about the health benefits that juices provide us. I hope you're as excited as I am!

Even though our health is one of the most important aspects of life, we tend to forget it amidst our hectic schedules and busy everyday endeavors.

Without good health, we cannot perform to our best potential. Poor health can hinder us from living life to the fullest.

Our usual excuse not to hit the gym or eat healthy, home-cooked meals is because of our hectic schedules and the lack of time – attending work/school, taking care of children and other activities that we do on a daily basis. Stressful, isn't it?

Well, I believe many would agree that the real key to living healthier is a change in lifestyle.

Changing Your Lifestyle: Ready for a Healthier Life?

I understand that this is easier said than done. Believe me, whenever I felt tired from work I would always resort to ordering in pizza for dinner.

When I felt stressed out, I would sit on my couch watching TV for hours, stuffing myself with junk foods. I didn't exercise because I thought I had no time. But later on my body was sluggish and I frequently got sick– that was when I decided I needed a lifestyle change.

You don't have to change all your old habits and daily routine right away. It's okay to start small.

One great way to start your healthy lifestyle is to eat or consume your much-needed vitamins and nutrients efficiently and consistently. This means that your diet must be balanced, your food must be easy to find and quick to prepare, and wastes no time in your busy everyday schedule.

This is why juicing is a wonderful way to become healthier and thus, more productive, without hating the taste of what you consume.

Although whole fruits and vegetables are very good for your health and to stay fit as well, they take time and effort to prepare. But once you learn the ropes, it will be a smooth-sailing path for a healthier you.

If you purchase your choice fruits and vegetables in the morning, you always get the best and freshest selection, which is quite important. Fresh organic fruits and vegetables from your local market pack a lot of power in boosting up your energy throughout the day.

Plus, the body loves juicing. You immediately feel a lot better within days of starting to juice. Juice is refreshing and can be consumed on a consistent basis without side effects to the body, unlike, say, eating cheeseburgers and fries everyday for one week.

I know you suddenly craved those two popular items just from me writing down the words, but imagine their effects on your health. The grease, oils, extenders, processed chemicals and all that nasty, unnatural stuff (ugh!) can seriously harm your body in the long run.

Food cravings and the idea of dieting or staying on a diet are big problems for many people. Cravings can hit hard when you least expect them,, hence my burger and fries quip.

A lot of people find difficulties in sticking to healthy eating because of these cravings (especially men), but when you replace steaks (here I go again) and other such high fat foods with fresh juices that are extracted from fruits and vegetables, you'll be surprised to find out that your body stops craving "bad" things.

Then, you will be able to convince your body and your mind, too, to follow a different path and in turn, you will gain vital nutrients instead. Now, that's a road very few follow.

The Health Benefits of Fruit and Vegetable Juices

Now, back to juicing and its benefits.

Perhaps you can replace your fast food with beets and its leaves, sweet potatoes, apples, oranges, pineapples and the like, which are fruits and vegetables that we forget are living things that can give us a whole lot of energy.

Some might even be surprised that once they start a juicing program of detoxifying, they might have difficulty sleeping at the beginning. This is because juicing packs you with vitamins and minerals that will have you bursting with energy from those nutrients. The benefits do not end with just that.

Given that you follow a good program (specific juicing recipes) and are disciplined, juicing can perform many more wonders for you like sharpening your mind and relieving you of body pains due to strenuous activities.

Specific recipes can focus on giving you better memory to help you perform tasks better.

Other recipes can give you the power to perform like an athlete by nourishing your muscles. Certain recipes also help improve your eyesight, skin, and even hair and nails, basically your overall general appearance. Others have anti-aging benefits. You can lose weight and tone up as well. This is the so-called glow others see in fit, healthy people who follow the right diet and exercise.

Juicing provides an equal amount of benefits to your body internally as well as externally. The antioxidants and other nutrients that fruit and vegetable juices contain detoxify your insides, flush out harmful elements and toxins, giving the body a good, clean start.

It is also said that juicing can help reduce the risk of cancer due to this cleansing and getting rid of toxins from the body. The elements found in vegetables contain and suppress bad bacteria within the body and replace them with good bacteria.

Typically, compared to meat and even fruit, people do not eat enough vegetables. Ideally, vegetables should be consumed regularly and at each meal. So, one of the great benefits of juicing is when you juice vegetables, the fiber gets separated and your body can absorb the bulk of the nutrients it needs from the juice. Although there are some benefits derived from fiber, the most important and most helpful vegetable nutrients come from the juice.

This also helps the digestive system rest from working too hard to digest fiber. As I mentioned earlier, since juicing removes the indigestible fiber, vital nutrients are available to the body in much larger quantities compared to eating whole fruits and vegetables.

For comparison, when you eat a raw carrot, you are only able to absorb about 1% of the available beta carotene, since many of the available nutrients from the carrot are stuck in the fiber.

Conversely, if a carrot is juiced, removing the fiber in the process, almost 100% of the beta-carotene can be absorbed by your body. That difference is actually as shocking as it is significant.

Typically, if you juice vegetables alone, you might think it wouldn't taste too good. Some people refuse to try living a healthy lifestyle due simply to the shallow reason that they think their taste buds will be deprived of good-tasting food and drinks. I won't lie, it's true.

That is why what I recommend is to experiment which types of produce taste good to you personally when mixed. Be creative – there are hundreds of fruits and vegetables out there as well as thousands of juice recipes. I'm sure you can find many that your taste buds will approve right here in this book.

In addition to tasting yummy, another benefit of fresh juice is that it is a tremendous source of enzymes. In fact, these enzymes are one of the key benefits of drinking freshly-made juices.

Heat kills these valuable enzymes. When you eat vegetables, fruit or grain cooked at temperatures higher than 114 degrees (F), the heat destroys all the healthful benefits of their enzymes

Since vegetables and fruits are always juiced raw, all the enzymes are still present and potent when you consume these fresh juices. By keeping them intact, you get a healthier and more power-boosting meal to start your day.

Now I will explain the specifics of the benefits for your knowledge. The significance of this is what the enzymes in fresh juice bring you. Researchers and nutritionists are focusing on the presence of many micronutrients called phytochemicals.

Phytochemicals are substances that can help build or activate your much-needed enzymes. The enzymes, in turn, play an active role in protecting your cells from damage.

To further add to this and to state more benefits of juicing, you must know that fruit and vegetable juices are also good sources of the traditional nutrients that we usually see on vitamin bottles' labels. Oranges, lemons, grapefruit, and the like, which are citrus fruits, as well as fruits like strawberries, provide good portions of vitamin C, which provides plenty of health benefits to the body.

On the other hand, Carrot juice contains huge amounts of another popular nutrient – vitamin A in the form of beta-carotene. Furthermore, some green juices are a good source of vitamin E.

Fresh fruit juices are also good sources of very important and very helpful minerals such as potassium, iron, sodium, copper, magnesium and iodine, which are bound by the plant in a form that is most easily assimilated during digestion.

Yet another thing is that fruits and vegetables provide one more substance that is often overlooked, but is absolutely essential for good health. It is called water!

Yes, the so-called source of all life actually makes up more than half our body. Most of the cells in your body are made of water (65% or higher). In some tissues like your brain for instance, there are cells that are made up of 80% water as well.

As you certainly know by now from every article you have read about health and nutrition, water is absolutely necessary for good health, but you also know that most people don't drink or consume enough water per day, which is the popular 8 glasses a day.

Let's face it. Many of the fluids we do drink on a regular basis like tea, coffee, soft drinks, alcoholic drinks and artificially flavored beverages all contain varied substances your body must eliminate by excreting extra water, which can lead to dehydration.

On the other hand, fresh fruit and vegetable juices do not contain these unneeded and very unnatural substances and instead are full of pure, clean water that is good for you in every way.

The question now is when should you start juicing? Usually, we tend to seek validity by following trends. So far, attempts to promote the health benefits of juicing fruits and vegetables have only reached a relatively small part of society, despite being around for quite a long time.

The answer is **right now**!.

More and more articles and books are being written about both the short-term and long-term health benefits of juicing fruits and vegetables, such as this one, obviously. This is because juicing has been proven to be an effective way to boost your health.

People now know more about making crucial dietary changes as well, and realize the trend of juicing fruits and vegetables can provide real health benefits.

I believe the increasing popularity of the term "juicing" itself will continue to help more people, like it helped me.

The Secret Behind Losing Weight Through Juicing

Okay, now that you know the various wonderful benefits of juicing, the cherry on top is it can also help you lose weight. Amazing, I know! On this next stop of our journey, we will be focusing on fitness.

We've been called many things as a country. I've heard things like "the land of cheeseburgers" or "the land of the obese."

Yes, I am talking about this nagging, apparently always ever-growing problem of excess weight. In a place where 1/3 of the people are obese and 2/3 are overweight, it is difficult to go against the current, so to speak. Luckily for you (and for me, too!) now we know that juicing is the perfect way to start losing weight.

Not only is juicing a legitimate way to increase your vitality and your stamina, but it is also a tasty and refreshing solution to really help you in your weight loss goals and aims. It's like hitting two birds with one stone!

Weight Loss Benefits of Juicing

Juicing your fruits and vegetables can support your fat burning and weight loss goals in different and interesting ways, given that you do it properly, of course.

Pair juicing with regular and disciplined exercise and you are well on your way to the best shape you've ever been in your life!

Juicing supports such goals by doing things to your body like jump-starting your metabolism and thus decreasing your cravings for junk food. Another benefit is that juicing saturates your cells with bio-available nutrients. Lastly, it supports your body's natural fat-burning processes. This means flushing toxins stored in your fat cells and reducing acidity in your body, which in turn will burn your fat.

Oh, those cravings!

Usually, what causes your cravings for huge portions of food and sweets is that the body tends to starve for nutrients that are should be part of your regular diet. That is the reason you crave specific foods in the first place.

The unfortunate thing is that most modern day diets do not contain the nutrients your body desperately needs to stay healthy. This results in an increase in your food cravings. This is because your body is attempting to fill its nutritional voids, but junk food is the wrong answer to these cravings.

Dos and Don'ts of Juice Combinations

The "old-new" trend we know as juicing actually has its roots in strict, basic nutritional fact. The basic idea here is that fruits and vegetables have the vitamins and minerals and other much-needed elements you need to become and stay healthy and fit.

As I mentioned in the last chapter, once you change your currently unhealthy diet you will already be changing your lifestyle.

It makes perfect sense to replace your cheeseburgers and fries with different and healthier juice combinations. Do it. Do it whether you are trying to lose weight or just to feel better.

Lots of juice combinations contain antioxidants that can help boost your immune system and general health. Of course, note that losing weight is not great if it isn't done in a healthy and correct way.

Here are some easy tips you can follow to help you juice yourself into the best shape you can be in.

- Of course, juicing, like any other endeavor, is easier if you love what you are doing, consuming, etc. Look for juice combinations that you like. Save yourself from suffering and later complaining by downing heavy, purely vegetable combinations. As you go along and learn more about juicing, you will gradually explore and recognize which fruits and vegetables go together to satisfy your the tastes of your palate.

- Always remember to go organic. This just means organic products translate into organic juices. You should definitely do this strictly to avoid pesticides and other potentially harmful chemicals in your juices. You may want to keep the pulp and the nutrients in and get rid of the extra coatings and waxes of your fruits. The reason is that by doing this, you will have healthier results from juicing.

- Instead of consuming high-calorie fruits, replace them with vegetable juices. Do not underestimate the huge difference this can make. You might want to check out the caloric value of a banana compared to a carrot, just to put things into perspective (1 medium banana has 105 calories, while 1 medium carrot has 52 calories). An even better fact is that vegetables can add bulk to your juice without adding a boatload of calories that won't help your weight loss regimen much.

- You can also use thyroid helpers and fat burners if you want. Adding enzymes, specific metabolic elements or even simply a good dose of fiber can help weight loss . When you make up recipes for your juices, keep these additional elements in mind.

- A fun way to go, too, is to add some spices into the mix. Doing this will stimulate your metabolism. The common reaction might be that it seems a little out of place at first, but spices like cayenne pepper, cardamom or allspice and others like these can actually give your metabolism that extra boost. A good technique of adding spices to your juice combinations is to grind a small amount into the mix, gradually increasing until you like the new taste.

Later on in our journey I will discuss with you more detailed fruit and vegetable juice combinations to help you get started with living healthy while losing weight.

The Right Way to Do It

While the juice combinations for your diet are already very helpful in shedding those pounds you hate, you also must consider the way you go about preparing and drinking your juices. Here are some great ways to do it right so that you can lose weight faster.

- You should invest in a good juicer. Look at it this way. If you make your own juice at home rather than buying already mixed juice in bottles from your local store, you will spend the same money anyway, but you will be able to cut down on sugar and preservatives.

- The best blends include fruits such as grapefruit, strawberries, oranges, juicy berries and plums. Tomatoes and cucumbers are also good to use. Once you've picked the ones you like, dilute the juice with water by a third and then add lime juice or lemon juice (both are good) to help preserve your blends when you put them in the fridge. It's important not to add sweeteners to your juices.

- Always start your day with a nutritious breakfast. You can include whole wheat toast, some eggs, whole grain cereal, low fat milk and of course, your juice. It is very important to eat a good breakfast meal everyday of your juicing diet.

- For lunch and dinner, you should eat approximately half or 1/3 of what you normally ate in your old diet. Replace the balance with your juice. It may seem difficult to adjust at first, so if you get hungry in between meals, snack on vegetables or fruits as well.

- If you really want to keep burning those calories and have a significant weight loss, keep a regular exercise schedule while you are on your juicing diet. This can really help you meet your weight loss goals.

A fair warning and a smart tip, though. Always, always, always consult nutritionists and doctors before you start juicing. Although juicing is great for many, there is a possibility that it might not be the right path for you.

Healthcare experts can, most of the time, point you in the right direction when it comes to diet and nutrition. So know your information, and step in the right direction of weight loss!

Juice Fasts: Good or Bad?

What Are Juice Fasts and How Can They Help?

In the previous chapters, we saw how juicing can help improve your health as well as your fitness if you can incorporate it into your diet and daily routine. In this part of our journey, we will delve deeper into the wonders of the science that is juicing.

As mentioned earlier, juicing can be a part of your everyday life. What if I tell you, though, that it can be taken a step further and let it stand alone as a diet? Yes, you read that right. Your juicing continues, but your food consumption stops. This is called juice fasting.

Also sometimes referred to as juice cleansing, juice fasting is a method of fasting and detoxification. If and when you decide to do this, remember that you can only consume vegetable and fruit juices.

You are only allowed to obtain your nutrition from these juices, meaning that you are abstaining from solid food consumption. Although its health benefits are still being sorted out, results have been quite positive and encouraging.

Compared to a water fast, a juice fast helps the body to heal itself faster by accelerating the elimination of uric acid and several other inorganic acids from your body. Not to mention that the sugars found in fruits and vegetables strengthen your heart.

When Dr. Paavo Airola, PhD, ND, author of the book called "Juice Fasting", and a firm believer in juice fasts being used as effective treatments for various illnesses, was asked, "Is juice fasting a real fast or just a liquid diet?" he responded: "Any condition when your body is encouraged to initiate the process of autolysis, or self-digestion, is fasting. During juice fasting, when no solid foods, proteins or fats are consumed, your body will decompose and burn all the diseased and inferior protein and fat tissues, just as it does during a water fast. Juices are absorbed directly into the bloodstream without the usual process of digestion."

It is clear that juice fasts are much more powerful than water fasts, which have been used for thousands of years for cleansing, detoxing and treating all sorts of diseases. Juice fasts became increasingly popular only in the last century.

Juice fasts may last from a few days to several weeks, depending on the diet or choice of the participant. Let me remind you and do not forget this: The juice you must consume during a juice fast IS NOT the type of juice that is available commercially.

It is rather the type produced from freshly juiced organic fruits and vegetables. So don't get them confused or you will not benefit and your fast and effort will be in vain.

Typically, the primary reason why people pick up juice fasting is to lose weight. What most people don't know is that juice fasting can also be done for the purpose of stopping habitual behavior. These habitual behaviors include smoking, drinking soda, over-consumption of food and caffeine addiction, to name a few.

Some people even have many different reasons why they juice fast. Some use it as an alternative medicine. Some even believe it can heal chronic pain, cure cancer, depression and arthritis. Others believe that juice fasting can help heal specific organs and systems in the body.

No matter which health condition you want to address, juice fasting can be beneficial. These two chapters aim to show you how juice fasting can help and what happens during the process. Of course, first of all, you have to want to do it, because any type of fasting requires desire and commitment.

That, of course, follows the determination to lose weight, to be healthy and to improve in general. Simply put, juice fasting can not only help you lose weight, it can also help you attain a better quality of life, so that's the best of both worlds.

Whatever your situation may be, or whatever your motivation may be for doing this, the secret is to actually start doing it and the potential will turn into results. Here are some of the benefits from juice fasting that await you once you decide and begin.

Juice Fasts for Weight Loss

Juice fasting is good for losing weight. Using only juice from fruits and vegetables will help you lose weight very quickly and efficiently. During the first week of your new diet, you can lose up to 10 pounds very easily. Note that a lot of your initial weight loss will be water weight.

It is lost pounds, nonetheless, which is a very good start for your weight loss program. After the first week, though, you will lose between half a pound to a pound per day. It will depend on your level of activity and the quantity of the juice you drink.

Also, the weight you lose will depend on the length of your fast. For example, a 30-day juice fast can help you lose between 25 to 40 pounds. There have also been claims by people that they lost even more, with a few claiming to have lost 60 pounds.

The numbers will also be affected depending on how your body is made, so check up on your body type. Losing that half pound to a pound per day is already an indication of success. Anything more than that will already be a bonus for you.

Juice Fasts for Cleansing and Detoxification

Another benefit of juice fasting is detox cleansing. The juices cleanse your body (especially the digestive system) of harmful and disease-causing toxins. Plus, the nutrients found in fruits and vegetables have the ability to significantly boost your immune system, which can help your body fight disease.

In many cases, juicing has relieved the major symptoms of an illness like arthritis. Some people even claim to have been cured, There is nothing to lose if you juice fast. There are only positive things to gain like better health and fitness.

There have been countless accounts of promotion and claims about the benefits of juice fasting. With the increased cost of medication and healthcare, as well as ongoing increases in water, air and food-based bacteria and toxins, it is especially timely now to adapt this new lifestyle

More and more people are looking for more natural ways of fighting or preventing sickness, and juice fasting is by far one of the best and fastest ways of achieving that goal.

What Exactly Happens During A Juice Fast?

The next thing we will be talking about is how a juice fast works. In a nutshell, juice fasting is the substitution of solid food consumption in favor of the consumption of raw fruits and vegetables manually liquefied or juiced in a juicer.

A liquid diet followed for as little as 24 hours to 100 days or longer can be considered a juice fast. You must note, however, that the length of the fast depends on the purpose for which it is being done, and on the goals of the person doing the fast. Some people even try to juice fast for as long as a year for the purpose of wanting to be healed of certain chronic illnesses.

People who go on extended juice fasts don't purely use juice fasting. Some add soy protein powder, liquid multivitamin supplements, etc. to their diets to make sure all their nutritional needs are being met.

The usual way of doing a juice fast is to substitute a glass of freshly made juice in place of a meal like lunch or dinner on any given day.

The choice of how you fast is up to you. You may prefer to juice once or twice a week, or try intermittent fasting by juicing three days a week, then eating for the other four days. It all depends on your preference – you hold the reins!

During the process, everything depends on your schedule and availability, which is understandable and logical. You can always tell yourself you don't have enough time to juice, but that is not a sufficient excuse, though, to not start a juicing program or for stopping your current program because there is and will always be an appropriate juice fasting program that suits you and your schedule. You just have to look for it.

There really are no excuses. Whatever you're available to do is fine. Even juicing one day per month is better than not doing it at all. Given that availability itself already requires planning and effort, it is safe to say that this entire process requires work and discipline.

You need to buy your fruits and vegetables, wash them, peel and prepare them for juicing. Equally important is that you will need to buy or own a good juicer. The cleaning process after you juice can also be a little tedious. The pulp in fruits and vegetables can leave a mess!

If you're willing to do all this and tolerate these minor inconveniences in exchange for the amazing health and quick weight loss benefits juice fasting will always give you, then you have chosen smartly and correctly.

What else happens during juice fasting?

The Trick in the Process

The trick is to give you a chance to slow down and rejuvenate first. Let's face it, nowadays, the world we live in demands a fast pace, thus it has become harder to slow down in order to learn, practice and implement new and unique ways to improve our lives.

Fasting is one technique to improve health that's been overlooked before, even if it argues such results as improvement in physical, emotional and mental health!

In recent years, fasting has gained credibility, though. Research has shown that abstaining from solid food for a certain time can improve overall health and well-being, as well as improve anti-aging and life extension.

Stop and think for a second about the billions and billions of dollars being spent on anti-aging, on skin care, especially on weight loss and other "self-improvement processes." You should realize that by going through this process of juice fasting, and making it a habit, and then a lifestyle, you can achieve all your goals quickly, cheaply and naturally.

Full Healing Effect

Not many people know this, but almost all diseases start in the digestive tract. Some experts would even say simply that all diseases originate there. More prone to this danger are persons who are about twenty pounds overweight or more and especially those who eat poorly. Those who suffer from binge-eating are especially susceptible.

Juice fasting, though, whether you juice fruits, vegetables or a combination of both, is a surefire way to improve and even eventually heal potentially life-crippling conditions.

Juice fasting, when done the right way with the proper discipline, has potential to heal the entire being: body, mind and spirit. When detoxification occurs in your body, in turn, your mind becomes more alert and sharper.

It's no surprise for persons who juice fast regularly to claim that they think more clearly, function better and have more energy than they can use. During this process, they tend to forget depression and anxiety.

Foolproof Guide to Choosing the Best Juicer

Now that you know all about juice fasts, you won't be quite ready to start yet until you have a good juicer.

It's easy to say that any juicer would do as long as it does the job. But let me say that if you really want to reap the benefits of juice fasting, then you should invest in a good juicer. It's for your health and wellness, after all.

One major element that is often overlooked but very critical to the quality of your results is the juicier you to use. What is the point in grabbing the best available fruits and vegetables to juice if your juicer will not perform well enough to extract all the proper nutrients you need from the fresh ingredients you have bought?

This chapter will focus on what you need to look for in finding the best juicer for you, considering availability, price and performance.

You would be surprised by how many different types of juicers are out on the market today. I also used to think that a juicer was just a juicer and nothing more, but years ago when I started my first juice fast I learned that different types of juicers cater to different needs.

In my opinion, there isn't one "best juicer" out there that fits everyone's needs. What's important is that you choose one that fits yours and will serve you well personally.

Types of Juicers and Their Pros and Cons

There are mainly 5 types of juicers and each has its own pros and cons. Weigh each pro and con carefully to determine which type of juicer will work best for you.

Centrifugal Juicers

One of the most popular choices, a centrifugal juicer is good for juicing soft fruits and hard vegetables. It is an ideal choice for first-time juicers and those who are on a budget.

This type of juicer has a fast, rotating blade that produces a centrifugal force which shreds your fruit and vegetables instantly and ejects the pulp and juice into separate containers.

46

Pros

- Usually on the low end of the price range

- Good for juicing produce with large surfaces (most fruits and hard-root vegetables)

- Less prep work because they have large openings so you won't have to cut your produce as much

- Works fast

- Easy to clean

Cons

- Not ideal for juicing leafy greens

- Not very efficient with extracting juice from pulp

- Fast action may produce foam

- Heat of high speed centrifugal force oxidizes the juice more and destroys some enzymes

- Loud

Some good centrifugal juicers include the Jack Lalanne Juicer, the Breville Juice Fountain series and the Omega 4000.

Masticating (Single Gear) Juicers

Also sometimes referred to as the "single auger" juicer, the masticating juicer is ideal for crushing and grinding fruits, veggies, leafy greens and even nuts – it can even double as a food processor as it is capable of mincing nuts and veggies.

It crushes the produce, extracts the pulp into separate containers and squeezes out the juice.

Pros

- Excellent at juicing leafy greens and vegetables
- Produce a drier pulp meaning it extracts more nutrients from the produce
- Durable (usually comes with warrantees of 10 years or more)
- Can be used to make fruit sorbet, baby food, nut butters, sauces etc.
- Quieter than centrifugal juicers
- Easiest to clean of all juicers

Cons

- Not very ideal for soft fruits
- Work slower than centrifugal juicers
- Usually have smaller openings which means more prep work
- Take up the most counter space compared to other types of juicers

Some good masticating juicer models you could consider are the Omega 8004, Omega 8006 and the Champion brand juicers.

Triturating (Twin Gear) Juicers

This type of juicer is my personal favorite because it is very versatile. Triturating juicers are high-end juicers that have two interlocking screws that crush and grind the produce. It works similarly to the masticating juicer but slower and more efficient.

Pros

- Efficient in juicing all types of produce – soft or hard fruits and vegetables, nuts and leafy greens
- Produces the driest pulp which means more juice and more nutrients
- Can be used to make fruit sorbet, nut butters, baby food, sauces, pasta etc.
- Pulls the produce in with minimal effort
- Upright design takes up less counter space

Cons

- Expensive
- Requires more effort to clean

The Green Star brand juicers and the Omega Vert 350 are some triturating juicers worth checking out.

The other two types of juicers are the citrus and wheatgrass juicers. They are both designed to juice a specific type of produce.

The citrus juicer is specialized to juice citrus fruits such as lemons, oranges, limes and grapefruit while obviously, the wheatgrass juicer is designed to efficiently juice wheatgrass.

Unless you are planning to juice just these types of produce, I don't recommend that you buy separate juicers as all of these can be juiced using any of the 3 types of juicers I mentioned above.

Important Tips When Buying a Juicer

So how do you know what juicer is best for the price you can pay? Here are some of the most important things to look for:

Ease of Operation

Let's face it. No matter how excited you are to start or continue your juicing program, like any endeavor, if it becomes tedious to the point that you force it, you will either stop doing it or you will not do it as often as you are required to.

A very important thing to look for in a juicer is how easy it is to use and how easy it is to clean afterwards.

Speed and Power

If you are looking for a quality juicer, you should buy one with a machine which has at least 1/4 horsepower to do its job properly. This is very important because sometimes, going cheap will make you give up some quality. Some cheaper juicers tend to have less power in their machines.Lower powered juicers have the tendency to leave some juice in the pulp. Also, this means that if your juicer is overworked to compensate for its lack of power, it may wear out more quickly.

Of course, you also need to consider the speed at which your juicer operates. The faster it works, the more time you save and the more juice you get. It's as simple as that.

Quality of Juice

The quality of juice a juicer makes is an important consideration. Remember that you will be juicing both fruits and vegetables.

Creating quality juice means that your end product must have a high nutrient and high enzyme content, and low quality juicers tend to smash fruits and vegetables in such a way that some beneficial chemicals in the juice are broken down by the heat produced by the juicing mechanism

Furthermore, some juicers spin so fast that they tend to give a higher oxidation rate (think centrifugal juicers.) More oxygen makes juice spoil faster.

You must look for a juicer with the right balance of features to handle the fruits and vegetables you prefer to juice and still produce high nutrient juices. In short, buy an efficient machine.

Yield per Pound

Note this: This attribute is what really separates the best juicers from the rest. Delving into a more technical side, you must know that a good juicer extracts more juice per pound compared to cheaper juicers.

Let's put it this way: You may be able to save about a hundred dollars right now by purchasing a cheaper model, but every time you juice, you will be throwing money away because you are getting less juice from your fruits and vegetables.

Obviously, in time, the money will catch up to the quality. An indication of a good juicer is that it can get up to 25% more juice per pound compared to most cheap, lesser quality juicers. This means that if you get the cheaper juicer, in about a year, the hundred dollars you saved at the time of purchase will literally go down the drain, and from that point on you will be losing money!

Lasting Power

With most products that you buy, you almost always get what you pay for. Of course, good quality products come with quality warranties.

A lot of the juicers available in the market at a cheap price (usually under $100) boast cheap motors that do not handle seeds, cores and rinds well. With such a juicer, every piece of fruit and/or vegetable must be sliced in tiny pieces so that the motor of your juicer does not burn out.

Unfortunately, the best way to go is to choose quality over price and the best juicers, the ones I recommend, start at a price range of $300 or higher, although you can often find them on sale for far less.

The Right Way to Prepare Your Fruits and Vegetables for Juicing

You know why you want to undergo a juice fast. You know which juicer to buy. But no, you are still not quite ready to begin just yet.

I know you're as excited as I am but first, in this part of our journey we will discuss something every first-time juicer should learn – the right way of preparing your produce for juicing.

The first most important thing to keep in mind is to use only organic fruits and vegetables. Why? This is because non-organic fruits and vegetables usually contain plenty of agricultural chemicals, bacteria, pesticides and parasites. Sometimes these unwanted chemicals are also present even in organic produce.

It is vital to make sure that we don't get any of these harmful chemicals into our system. We are after all, trying to cleanse and detoxify – not the other way around. Getting rid of all the bacteria and parasites won't be easy, but with proper means and techniques, it can be done.

The most common method of cleaning and detoxifying fresh produce is to add 4 teaspoons of salt and 4 teaspoons of lemon juice in a sink full of cold water. You then soak the fruits and vegetables in the mixture and rinse. Others opt to boil their produce, but this method isn't exactly ideal for fruits and for leafy greens.

If you want to clean your produce in a simple and traditional way like I do, here are some steps you can follow:

Step 1

Gather all the fruits and vegetables you are planning to use and place them in a colander. Bring the colander into the sink under the faucet.

Step 2

Run your produce under the water. It is not advisable to use hot or freezing water when washing your produce. You can use a brush to clean harder fruits and vegetables such as carrots and potatoes, but make sure to use a brush with soft bristles to avoid digging into the skin.

Step 3

Make sure that no dirt is left on your fruit and vegetable surfaces. Gently cut off any bad spots.

Step 4

The FDA doesn't recommend using soap, detergent or other cleaning agents when washing fruits and vegetables but I like using gentle soaps to wash my produce.

Food-safe soaps and cleaners can be found in health food stores and markets. I use these cleaners to remove oil-based residues that are not water-soluble like pesticides, waxy preservatives and other oils.

Step 5

Once you are done washing your produce, peel everything that needs to be peeled and cut up everything that needs to be cut up and then you're good to go!

Fruits vs. Vegetables

Before you start juicing your way to a healthy weight loss, I'd like to discuss with you the most important part of your new diet, aka juice fast– fruits and vegetables.

Since we were young we were always told to eat fruits and vegetables because they would make us strong and healthy. Well, our parents and teachers couldn't be more right – fruits and vegetables are the healthiest foods around.

We have already discussed in the previous chapters the various health benefits that fruit and vegetable juices give us as well as how they can help us shed extra pounds.

In this part of our journey we will focus mainly on the produce; but first I'd like to share with you some fun, useful facts about fruits and vegetables.

- Technically speaking, a fruit is the sweet and fleshy part of a plant, surrounding the seeds. They are actually the ripened ovaries of plants.

- Vegetables are cultivated for an edible part which means that all other edible parts of a plant are vegetables as well.

- Vegetables are often categorized as foods that are part of the main course of a meal, while fruits are reserved for snacks and dessert.

- Most fruits are sweet (giving the notion that they are for dessert) because of their fructose content. Vegetables contain much less fructose, thus their lack of sweetness.

- Here are some fruits that are commonly mistaken as vegetables: cucumbers, corn kernels, eggplants, tomatoes, avocados, squashes, pumpkins, zucchini, peapods, olives and green, red and yellow peppers.

One thing that fruits and vegetables have in common is that they are both packed with essential vitamins and minerals as well as phytochemicals.

Phytochemicals are powerful naturally occurring substances that protect plants from weather damage, pests and disease. They are also responsible for giving plants their vibrant colors.

When we consume fruits and vegetables, we also reap the benefits of phytochemicals, including immunity boost and protection against chronic diseases. Individually, though, fruits and vegetables have their own set of health benefits to offer us.

Benefits of Fruits

Often referred to as "nature's perfect food" by health experts, fruits offer a myriad of health benefits (aside from being yummy!) They are as follows:

- Low in fat but loaded with fiber and water which promotes healthy digestion.

- Have low sodium content but are high in natural sugars which makes them a healthier choice compared to processed snacks.

- Contain nutrient-dense calories which supply our body with vitamins, minerals and energy.

- Citrus fruits are rich sources of Vitamin C. Kiwis, papayas and mangoes are also packed full of powerful antioxidants which help protect against cancer, heart disease and eye problems.

- Fruits like melons are packed with essential minerals such as calcium (bone health) and potassium (muscle strength and metabolism of fats and protein).

Benefits of Vegetables

The term "vegetable" comes from the Latin word "vegetare" which means "to animate or enliven" and I think that says it all.

Like fruits, they are nutrient-dense foods that give our body countless health benefits.

- Low in fat and sodium but have high fiber and water content.

- Low in natural sugars compared to fruits; that's why they are often used and recommended for weight loss or weight maintenance diets.

- Brightly-colored vegetables provide antioxidants, Vitamins A and C and selenium which fight against free radical damage.

- Leafy greens are a rich source of chlorophyll which detoxifies the liver and promotes healthy digestion.

- Broccoli, Brussels sprouts and cauliflower belong to what is called the cruciferous family and they are known to have powerful anti-cancer properties.

Should fruits and vegetables be juiced together?

While both fruits and vegetables provide equally good benefits and contribute to weight loss, it is not advisable that you combine them when juicing. This is mainly because they require different digestive processes. This goes for both consuming the produce raw or when juiced.

Those who have habitually consumed fruits and vegetables at the same time along with improper combinations of food experienced unexplained weight gain and a bloated, full feeling.

So when you are juicing, mix fruits with fruits and vegetables with vegetables to avoid unnecessary discomforts. There are exceptions, though, like celery and lettuce which could be combined with either a fruit or vegetable juice.

Fruits such as apples and small amounts of avocado, oranges and lemons are also safe to mix with vegetables when juicing – I add small amounts of fruits to my vegetable juices to sweeten them.

Juice Recipes for Weight Loss

Congratulations! Now that I have shared with you all you need to know about juicing, I think you are now ready to give it a try.

In light of this happy event, I would like to share with you some of my favorite recipes that I have gathered over the years.

There are thousands of fruit and vegetable juice recipes out there, but these are personally tried, tested and approved by me, my family and friends.

I took the liberty of categorizing the recipes into 5 categories to help you get off to a good start:

- fat-burning/weight loss juices,
- juices for detox,
- energy-boosting juices,
- vitaminizing juices,
- green juices

Let's begin with the fat burning juice recipes.

Fat-Burning Juices

The Ultimate Slimming Juice

When I am on a juice fast, I drink this power juice as a meal replacement for breakfast.

When I wake up in the morning, I drink a glass of warm water mixed with lemon before working out.

It is believed that working out in the morning with an empty stomach helps burn fat the best!

I drink this refreshing juice afterwards. It is designed to provide the body with essential amino acids, vitamins, minerals, fats, enzymes and water.

Take this 100% plant based meal twice a day as a meal replacement (no artificial flavors or sweeteners, refined sugars, dairy or saturated fats) and you'll surely see amazing weight loss results.

Ingredients:

2 apples

2 stalks of celery

1 peeled lime

3 cm chunk of ginger

1/3 medium cucumber

Optional: After you've juiced all the ingredients mentioned above, you can opt to turn this slimming juice into a slimming smoothie. Simply mix the juice with ½ ripe avocado and a small handful of ice into a blender then blend until you reach the desired smoothness.

The Green Machine

If you're a veggie lover then this is the perfect juice for you because it is heavy on greens. I concoct this yummy recipe when I want to take a break from sweet juices.

It is designed to boost your energy while helping your body lose weight.

I recommend you try this power juice if you're going to have a long day that requires a lot of energy.

Ingredients:

3 cucumbers

1 bunch of kale

1/2 bunch of parsley

1/2 bunch of spinach

1/2 bunch swiss chard

1 peeled lemon or lime

Note: *If you just started your juice fast and decided to go with this recipe, I suggest that you begin with a smaller quantity than I listed above – start off with half of the quantity for each ingredient.*

Green Carrot Juice

This is one of my favorite fat-burning juice recipes because I simply love carrots in my juices. Apart from helping the body lose weight, this green juice is designed to stimulate the nerves and improve energy.

It's also an effective breath-freshener and helps improve body odor.

This powerful green juice is packed with essential nutrients like Vitamins A, C and K, potassium, magnesium, iron, copper, manganese and chlorophyll.

Ingredients:

4 medium carrots

1 apple

1/2 peeled lemon

2 stalks of celery

1 handful of parsley

1 handful of spinach

Cantaloupe-Cinnamon Juice

If you're craving for something sweet, this is a weight loss juice to try. This refreshing and flavorful juice has high amounts of digestive enzymes, Vitamins A and C, antioxidants and myo-inositol (good for alleviating stress and insomnia).

This simple juice is also good for the eyes, the skin and the arteries. I concoct the cantaloupe-cinnamon juice when I want to take a break from vegetable juices. I like to add ice to make it even more refreshing.

Ingredients:

1 cantaloupe

Dash of cinnamon

5 ice cubes

Cucumber Protein Juice

When you're in a juice fast, especially during the first few days, you will be craving solid foods. This low-calorie juice is the perfect choice when that situation comes up, as its protein will help keep your hunger at bay.

Cucumber protein juice is packed full of sodium, pectin and silicon and is designed for weight loss. It also helps lower your cholesterol levels and is good for your hair, nails and skin.

Ingredients:

1 cucumber

1 apple

3 stalks of celery

2 tbsp. of vanilla protein powder (this can be purchased at your local health store)

Apple Berry Fiber

Fiber is known to help cleanse the system. This delicious fat-burning fruit juice is packed full of Vitamins C and E. I like to make this recipe on a hot, sunny day as it is simply refreshing.

Ingredients:

3 medium apples

1/4 cup fresh or frozen blueberries

1/2 cup fresh cranberries

1 tbsp. powdered psyllium (fiber)

Green Pineapple

Another refreshing slimming juice for a hot, sunny day, Green Pineapple is full of flavor. It provides lots of Vitamin C and is designed to revitalize the body and boost your energy.

Ingredients:

1 cup. of pineapple

1/2 cup. of broccoli

1/2 cup of cucumber

1 kiwi

Spiced Apple Juice

I have listed fat-burning juice recipes to drink for hot days, but what about on cold days? Well, this spiced apple juice is my top pick for cuddle weather.

Apples are known to promote weight loss and bone strength as well as help lower your cholesterol levels; and this relaxing drink helps you achieve just that.

Ingredients:

3 apples

1 pinch of cinnamon

Instructions: After juicing the apples, pour the juice into a saucepan and heat (do not boil). Pour into a mug, add the cinnamon and serve.

The Hunger Fighter

As I've mentioned before, one of the biggest challenges you will encounter when you're juicing for the first time is hunger.

Cravings for solid food are normal, that's why this recipe is something I would recommend when you find yourself wanting even just a piece of cracker.

Packed full of antioxidants, this juice is so refreshing that you'll forget why you even craved for something else in the first place.

Ingredients:

4 medium Carrots

3 Parsley Sprigs

2 small Apples

1 small Cucumber

The Vita-Slim Juice

If you're looking for something light, something to sip while you're busy working or relaxed watching your favorite TV show, this slimming juice is the perfect choice.

Rich in Vitamin C, this juice recipe is known to promote effective weight loss and healthy metabolism.

Ingredients:

1/2 cup fresh or frozen Strawberries

1 cup freshly-squeezed Orange Juice

1/2 Lemon

Note: *Use as many oranges as you need to get 1 cup of juice. Add a couple of ice cubes for a more refreshing twist!*

Juices for Detox

Purple Pine

This is a good healthy juice recipe to make for detoxification. This drink is high in Iron and can act as a potential anti-inflammatory and digestive agent. Drink this to feel great and rid your tummy of the toxins it does not need!

Ingredients:

1/2 Pineapple

1 full cup of Grapes (preferably Black Grapes)

Note: It is good to drink this juice after your lunch or after your dinner. Let it act as your dessert, instead of eating unhealthy and potentially harmful sweets. Grape juice is also known to be good for your heart.

The Body Cleanser

I found that the main benefits from this healthy juice recipe include good results such as body revitalization and better-looking and glowing skin.

Typically, beauticians will prescribe you this juice because of its easily-seen positive effects on the skin.

The main benefits of this recipe are not limited to the skin, though. This is one of the healthiest juice recipes out there. It boasts cleansing effects, boosting effects for the entire body.

Ingredients:

3 apples

1 inch of ginger

3 carrots

This recipe is a multi-benefit treat. It is good for the heart, skin, energy, detoxification and the overall betterment of your body.

The Cholesterol Buster

Although I'm listing juicing recipes that focus on detoxification and energy boosting purposes, this recipe is a top pick among all healthy juice recipes. This juice is known to help reduce cholesterol.

Not only that, it is kind of a detox juice because it improves any kind of stomach upset, as well as a headache remedy. This is especially good and a must for you if you have reached your thirties and want to live a healthy lifestyle.

Ingredients:

4 apples

2 cucumbers

2 stalks of celeries

Note: *For best results, you should drink this juice every other day the entire week!*

The Wild Thing

This healthy juice recipe is a favorite among juicing dieters because of its taste. Nonetheless, this mouth-watering treat is healthy and definitely good for you.

The Wild Thing cleanses both the bladder and the kidney of toxins that usually lurk in those organs. Not only that, but it also dispels excess salts from your body. It is an excellent detoxification juice.

Ingredients:

2 Apples

1/2 Pineapple

1/4 Watermelon

Note: Most people use a tint of salt with this recipe, but you can also choose to drink it as it is without the salt flavor. It is up to you. Also, you should remove the seeds of the fruits. Otherwise, the taste will be different.

The Vitamin J!

If you are looking for a significant energy boost, this is an extremely healthy choice because it has loads and loads of vitamins.

It should be a popular concoction with your kids, as well, (if you have any) because of its distinct good taste. It packs Vitamin C and Vitamin B2.

It also increases and powers cell activity, and strengthens immunity, giving you the energy to stay focused and energized the entire day.

It simply provides all the necessary vitamins you get from vitamin capsules and supplements, but in a more natural and healthier way.

Drinking this juice is absolutely better than taking those pills, which may have chemicals that are potentially harmful to your body.

Ingredients:

Honeydew

Black Grapes

Watermelon

Milk

Sample Proportion: Make this juice in whatever quantity you like, but always mix equal proportions of all the ingredients. For example, one cup each of honeydew, black grapes, watermelon and milk.

The Sugar Fighter

One of the simpler and easier recipes to remember, you must not ignore its usefulness. As easy as it is to remember, it is also easy to digest.

This particular healthy juice recipe targets and focuses on correcting irregularities in the amount of sugar in your blood. It regulates the sugar content in your body.

To remember this recipe, simply think Pear and Banana. Firstly, pears are good for problems with ulcers, constipation, and urination. They can also work for congestion, fever alleviation, and cough.

Secondly, bananas are good for lowering high blood pressure because of their low salt content. Furthermore, bananas contain tryptophan. It is a type of protein that our body converts into serotonin. Serotonin is a hormone known to make you feel happy and improve your mood.

This healthy juice recipe is best for people looking for a low-salt, detoxification juice that also helps you improve your sugar problems.

Ingredients:

3 Pears

2 Bananas

Note: *Juice as many Pears and Bananas you like, but just keep the 3:2 proportion.*

Anti-Oxidant Supreme

As its name suggests, this juice recipe will act as a great antioxidant for your body. It does a lot of good things for you such as clearing the body of heat, decreasing your blood pressure, counteracting toxicity in your body and the like.

Ingredients:

3 Mangoes

2 Pears

2 Carrots

2 Apples

Note: Adding apples to any healthy juice recipe is good because they are a very well-known antioxidant. The addition of the mango in this recipe just makes it very tasty, so you can drink it again and again.

Fruity Liver Lover

The liver is one of the most important organs responsible of detoxing, so if you want a healthy treat that effectively detoxifies your liver and your whole body, give this recipe a try.

It is loaded with a fiber called pectin, which helps cleanse the digestive tract and supports healthy liver detox.

Ingredients:

4 Apples

2 Lemons

1 Lime

Fruit and Tea Detox Juice

Aside from fresh fruits and vegetables, herbal tea is also known as an effective body detoxifier.

I always have a warm cup of herbal tea whenever I over-indulge and feel bloated after eating, so I thought of mixing it up with my juices for the same effect.

The best part is that herbal tea helps relieve anxiety and stress by providing a calming effect.

Drink this juice after a long, hectic day and you'll instantly feel better.

This juice recipe also helps detoxify the entire body, focusing on the kidneys. Dandelion root, nettle, ginger root and turmeric tea are great choices.

Ingredients:

1 Lemon

2 tbsp. All Natural Cranberry Juice

1 teabag Herbal Tea

Honey Lemon Detox Juice

The key to a successful juice fast is variety. This way, you won't feel like you're drinking the same thing over and over again.

What I do is alternate hot and cold juices. So if you feel like drinking something to warm you up (during winter months, maybe), this detox juice is a must-try.

As you know, lemons are known for many detox benefits. They are packed full of citric acid, calcium, magnesium, Vitamin C, bioflavonoids and many more and have anti-oxidant and anti-infection properties.

On the other hand, honey has anti-bacterial, anti-fungal and anti-inflammatory properties.

Ingredients:

1/2 tbsp. Raw Honey

1/2 Lemon

A pinch of Cayenne Pepper

1 cup Warm Water

Note: *You can also serve this drink cold. The honey-lemon detox juice is best consumed on an empty stomach.*

Energy-Boosting Juices

Road Runner Energy Boost

The name describes it best. If you drink this healthy juice recipe, you will be out and running like a Road Runner in no time. If you are the type who needs some kind of pep up every morning, this one is best for you.

You already know what Apples can do for your body, but the Ginger will help boost your blood circulation which helps with energy a lot. Also, the Ginger gives an edgy taste to your juice's flavor.

Ingredients:

8 medium Carrots

3 Apples

1 inch of Ginger

March to the Beet!

This recipe is very good for vitality. For those of you who are looking for the complete package when it comes to detox juices, this is as close as you can get. Plus it is very nice tasting, too.

Beetroot juice is very rich and this healthy juice recipe addresses that fact. The lime juice is added to help cut through the richness of the beet for a perfect balance.

An excellent source of iron and also Caretonoid Betaine, beetroot juice is a detox monster. Betaine has numerous benefits including antioxidant properties. It also helps with red blood cell production and lymph activity.

No less powerful, red peppers also contain an abundance of anti-oxidants, so this juice recipe can provide cancer preventive properties as well.

Adding yet more punch to this super detox recipe, pears are also a good source of soluble fiber and thus, can help 'sweep out' your intestines..

Ingredients:

1 medium Beetroot

1 handful Basil leaves

2 Pears

1 Lime

1/2 of a red Bell pepper, seeded

Directions: *Cut the top and tail of the Beetroot, then scrub it if it is organic or home grown, otherwise peel it and cut into pieces small enough to fit in your juicer.*

Wash the pears, peel the lime and wash and de-seed the pepper.

Fold the Basil leaves up tightly and feed them into the juicer between pieces of Beetroot.

Juice all the other ingredients, stir and drink it right away to keep it fresh!

Apple Spinach Parsley Lemon Juice

If you are the type of person running on a tight schedule, you may miss meals sometimes and that saps you of your much-needed energy to go a full day. But more importantly, it is unhealthy and this habit of missing meals will build toxins in your body as there is no food to digest.

This recipe is good for cleansing your insides and also most effective when consumed on an empty stomach.

Ingredients:

2 large Apples

1 medium handful of Spinach

1 small handful of Parsley

1/4 Lemon

Note: *Simply process all these ingredients together in your juicer and you are ready for cleansing and putting something in your tummy.*

This is a great detox juice that really helps cleanse your colon, as well.

Peter Piper's Pepper Punch

This juice recipe is great for boosting your immune system as it contains high levels of vitamin C to give you that energy you need for a full day's work.

Bell peppers are great sources of vitamin C. Any bell pepper would do, but red and yellow peppers contain twice as much vitamin C as green ones. All in all, they are all energy-boosting, whichever you prefer.

Ingredients:

2 Yellow Peppers

3 Oranges

2 Apples

2 Pears

1/2 Grapefruit

Directions: Thoroughly wash and de-seed the peppers and peel the oranges and grapefruit. Leave the pith on the citrus fruit as it contains Bioflavinoids which help the body absorb the vitamin C. Put all ingredients through the juicer and serve straight away. Serve it in 2 medium glasses.

Note: Some can find the flavor of green peppers a little bitter for their taste when used in juice recipes. The yellow peppers in this recipe are sweeter and melt into the other fruit flavors to give a subtle but definite taste.

Banana and Fig

To put it simply, your nervous system benefits from bananas and dates, while figs and raisins contain natural sugars to boost your energy.

Moreover, honey nourishes your stomach's digestion and gives you yet more energy!

Ingredients:

1 Banana (ripe)

4 Figs (sun-dried)

1 tablespoon of Honey

1 cup of Water

Note: *You can add a heaped teaspoon of bee pollen powder (or equivalent in capsules) to this healthy juice recipe for an extra boost, but it is optional.*

Egg Yolk & Carrot Juice

Another healthy juice recipe, good for energy-boosting, this one particularly focuses on improving blood quality, which in turn, helps relieve fatigue and gives you back your energy in no time. This is especially true for Carrot juice, which is also highly cleansing and nourishing.

Moreover, egg yolk stimulates sluggish, exhausted adrenal glands. Spirulina is a super-nutritious vegetable protein.

Ingredients:

1 large cup of freshly extracted Carrot juice

1 egg yolk

Note: *Add the egg yolk to the carrot juice then mix well with a fork. Add 1/2 a teaspoon of spirulina powder for an extra boost.*

Built for Taste

This certain juicer recipe imitates a famous soft drink with a popular tropical taste, but of course, leaves out the vast amount of added sugar and additives in the soft drink.

Pineapple plus Grapefruit is an excellent combo for a party in your taste buds.

This juice recipe is ideal if you think your system will need a vitamin C boost for energy as both Pineapple and Grapefruit are great sources of this antioxidant that is so effective at strengthening your immune system while keeping you sharp and strong.

Ingredients:

2 Grapefruits

1 Pineapple

2 small Apples

Note: *Look for heavy pineapples as this indicates a high water (and therefore juice) content. You may want to leave some piths of the Grapefruit as it helps the body absorb the Vitamin C that it needs for energy.*

Directions: Serve in 2 large glasses with ice.

Get-up-and-go Greens

This healthy juice recipe is an amazing energy enhancer. It is packed with vitamins, minerals and blood-purifying greens. It also contains beta-carotene and vitamin C found in Spinach and Kale, which also help with liver cleansing and support blood flow while boosting your energy.

Celery, on the other hand, is a very alkaline vegetable which helps with digestion. It also gives you a nice amount of calcium, magnesium and natural sodium, which together help transmit signals from your brain to your muscles to help them function properly, obviously a benefit to your energy levels.

And finally, ginger is excellent at helping reduce inflammation in the body, which improves your maneuverability

Ingredients:

1 Apple

3 Celery stalks

1 handful of Spinach

1 handful of Kale

1 inch slice of Ginger

Note: *This may not taste the best, so adding a Mango can help, but it is not recommended.*

Liver Detoxification Veggie Juice

This recipe is a mixture of fresh vegetables and fruits that have different unique flavors, but all help flush toxins from your body just fine. Pears, celery and cabbages are in fact the best liver detoxification agents available.

They help the liver function properly by inhibiting aggregation of fluid and toxins in the liver.

Ingredients:

1/4 Cabbage

1 Lemon

1 Celery stalk

1 inch Ginger Root

Filtered Water (500 ml)

5 leaves of fresh Mint

Note: Make sure all ingredients are fresh and drink the juice immediately after making it.

Sweet and Spicy Energy Juice

If you're in the mood for something zingy, this is the perfect juice to concoct. It's both refreshing and energizing, just what you need for a long day's work.

It's packed full with micronutrients that will keep your blood pumping and your energy levels high.

Ingredients:

2 medium Beetroots

1/2 Lemon

3 Cucumbers

1/2 inch Ginger

Note: The lemon will slightly diminish the powerfull beet flavor, while the ginger will give this juice a nice kick

Vitaminizing Juices

Asparagus Delight

Asparagus is low in calories and carbohydrates but high in protein. That's why it's good for when you start feeling hungry during your juice fast. Asparagus juices are also packed full of Vitamin C, folic acid and riboflavin.

One tip I can give you when shopping for asparagus is to look for ones with dark green stalks – the darker the stalk of the asparagus, the higher the nutrient content.

Ingredients:

4 asparagus spears

3 medium carrots

2 ribs of celery

Sweet Beets

Juices that use beet as an ingredient are vitamin-packed. Beets are rich sources of Vitamins A and C, calcium and iron. I always choose the smaller beets for juicing. I also always see to it that the beet roots are firm and intact, and that the beet tops are green and fresh.

Ingredients:

1/2 beet

1 sweet potato

2 medium apples

Orange Broccoli

Broccoli is known to be one of the most nutrient-dense foods. It has powerful anti-cancer effects and is packed with Vitamin C. Broccoli that has the highest concentration of nutrients are those that are dark green in color with purplish heads.

Ingredients:

1 spear of broccoli

2 medium carrots

2 apples

Sweet Brussels

This is one of my favorite simple green juices because I like Brussels sprouts a lot. Like broccoli, Brussels sprouts are high in Vitamin C, calcium, protein and phosphorus.

More importantly, the juice of Brussels sprouts has anti-cancer effects specifically known to lower the risk of breast cancer.

Ingredients:

4 Brussels sprouts

3 medium carrots

1/2 cup of spinach

1 small apple

Note: *Feed the Brussels sprouts into the juicer head first.*

The Morning Call

This recipe is a vitamin-packed juice that's good to have for breakfast. Cabbages are high in Vitamins C and E and sulphur.

Juices with cabbage in it help improve digestion and help reduce the risk of constipation.

Ingredients:

1/4 cabbage

1 or 2 broccoli (with stem)

4 kale leaves

Morning Combo Juice

I call this recipe the morning combo because I always drink this in the mornings, but of course you can concoct it any time of the day.

This refreshing drink is aimed to energize the body and to boost the immune system. As a side effect, you will also get glowing skin and stronger, healthier hair.

The recipe contains beetroot which is known to be an effective immune system-booster as well as a powerful antioxidant.

Apples, carrots and kale also have antioxidant properties. The ginger provides a twist to the recipe while providing its anti-cancer and anti-inflammatory benefits.

Lastly, the tropical twist of the lemon purifies the blood and helps prevent the risk of high blood pressure. All in all, this power-packed juice is what you need when you're feeling a bit under the weather.

Ingredients:

1 small Beetroot

1 Apple

2 small Carrots

1 bunch Kale

1 small Ginger Root

1/4 Lemon

Note: *When juicing the lemon, you can opt to include its rind to gain all the fiber it contains. If you wish to make the mixture sweeter, add another small apple.*

Berry Healthy

If you've had a long day then you deserve this treat of a juice.

Berry healthy is one of my favorites and my kids love it, too! Berries are not only known to be delicious, but they're extremely healthy as well. They are powerful antioxidants which protect the body from free-radical damage and against inflammation. These wonder fruits are also packed full of Vitamins A, C and E as well as fiber which not only makes you feel full, but also makes you eat less.

Best part of all these vitamins is that they are effective skin-beautifiers!

To gain the maximum health benefits that these nutrition powerhouses have to provide, consume 2-3 types of berries each day.

Ingredients:

1 cup Strawberries

1 cup Blueberries

1 cup Blackberries

1 cup Raspberries

Note: Don't forget to remove the stems before juicing the berries. You can also save the pulp of the fruits to eat later so they don't go to waste.

Sweet Orange Kick

Have you been feeling tired and sluggish all the time lately? This is an indication that you need your vitamins!

I remember making this juice every time I had to pull an all-nighter for work back in the days and it always worked like a charm.

The huge number of vitamins that is contained in citrus fruits (such as berries and oranges) provides the body with anti-bacterial, anti-inflammatory, anti-cancer and antioxidant benefits. Ginger promotes healthy digestion and because of this, the body can remove toxins which could be causing your sluggishness.

Ingredients:

3 Oranges

1 cup fresh or frozen Berries

1 inch Ginger Root

Note: Peel oranges and ginger root. For the 1 cup of berries, you have the freedom to choose which type of berry you'd like to juice.

Pineapple Play

This Pineapple Play is another vitaminizing juice recipe that will help you gain the energy you need for a long day.

I recommend this refreshing treat especially when you're about to do some physical work – may it be a busy weekend with the kids, some garage cleaning or some gardening. Pineapples and broccolis are excellent sources of Vitamin C.

A University of South Carolina research showed that consuming Vitamin C before and after some heavy physical work helps reduce sore muscles. Add a zesty twist to this recipe with the antioxidant and anti-inflammatory ginger root.

Ingredients:

1/4 medium Pineapple

4-5 Broccoli Stems

1/2 inch fresh Ginger Root

Note: You can add a handful of ice cubes to the juice to make the juice more refreshing.

Lunch Vitamix Juice

Lunch time is siesta time! So if you're feeling sleepy, lazy or plainly bored during noon time then knock yourself out with this delicious glass of fruity goodness.

The Lunch Vitamix Juice is a mixture of citrus fruits and bananas which will provide the body with a variety of vitamins and minerals. Citrus fruits are packed with energizing Vitamin C while bananas are rich in potassium.

This juice will help control your blood sugar levels and rehydrate your system on a hot day.

Ingredients:

1 Orange

1/2 cup Strawberries

1/2 cup Blueberries

2 Bananas

Note: You can add a handful of ice cubes if you prefer the drink cold. If you have time, throw the fresh juice into a blender and add 100 grams of low-fat white yogurt and some ice cubes for a mouth-watering smoothie!

Green Juices

Green for the Skin

When you're juice fasting, you are doing a detox/cleanse for your body as well. Due to the toxins being eliminated from the body, some beginners experience skin breakouts during the first day or two of the fast (don't worry this will eventually clear up). If you're conscious about your skin, here's a guaranteed juice recipe known for giving the skin a clear, healthy glow.

Cabbages are rich in Vitamin C, beta-carotene and selenium – all of which promote overall skin health. They also help slow down the skin's aging process.

Both the carrots and ginger have antioxidant properties, protecting our cells (including skin cells) against damage from free radicals.

Ingredients:

8 small Cabbage Leaves

3 large Carrots

1 inch fresh Ginger Root

Note: If you've been juicing fruit-based juices lately, break the ice with this yummy vegetable juice once in a while.

Garden Lemonade

Imagine the refreshing taste of fresh lemonade plus the health benefits of leafy greens. If that sounds great to you, you're in luck because that's exactly what you'll get from this green juice recipe.

Lemons provide powerful antioxidant Vitamin C while spinach provides Vitamin A, C, E, K and B Vitamins. Cucumbers and pears are rich in water, so they help rehydrate and replenish the body.

Ingredients:

3 cups Spinach

1 Cucumber

1 Lemon

1 Pear

Note: Peel the lemon and pear, but keep the skin of the cucumber. Throw in a handful of ice cubes into your glass for a unique lemonade experience.

Garden in a Glass

If you're not particularly fond of eating your leafy greens then this is the perfect juice for you.

Dark green leafy vegetables are loaded with chlorophyll, B complex vitamins, silicon and many other important nutrients. They are good for the body's general health.

Add fiber-rich apples and the tangy flavor of Vitamin C-rich tangerine and you'll definitely change your mind about leafy greens.

Ingredients:

8 Romaine Lettuce Leaves

4 Celery Stalks

1 big handful of Dark Leafy Greens (Kale, Parsley and Spinach)

1 Tangerine

2 Green Apples

Note: You can opt for a sweeter variety of apples for this recipe. Peel and de-seed the tangerine.

Kale All the Way

Another green juice recipe that I would recommend is Kale All the Way.

Personally, I love Kale – I consume it as much as I can whether mixed with my fresh juices or in a fresh salad. It is one the world's healthiest foods, containing about 45 antioxidant and anti-inflammatory flavonoids.

Celery, on the other hand, is another nutrition powerhouse, containing Vitamins A, C, K, B Vitamins, flavonoids, folate and many more.

Add carrots which are packed full of beta-carotene and a fiber-rich apple to sweeten things up.

Ingredients:

3 cups Kale

4 stalks Celery

2 small Carrots

1 medium Apple

Note: *If you'd like, you can add a small handful of other leafy greens like spinach, parsley and broccoli.*

Healthy Captain Crunch

Deciding to do a juice fast is one thing, committing to it is another. When your taste buds get bored of the same flavor, you'll likely break your juice fast and return to a less healthy lifestyle by eating foods you've been craving.

So when I say be creative with your juices, it's not merely just about alternating fruits and vegetables. One way you can do to maintain a healthy variety is to play around with texture as well.

Sometimes I like to sprinkle my green juices with chia seeds. These little superfoods are rich in fiber and Omega-3 healthy fats. They are known for boosting energy, lowering cholesterol levels and promoting healthy digestion among other benefits. And of course, they provide a little "oomph" to your green juices.

Ingredients:

1 cup kale

1 cup spinach

3 stalks celery

1 cucumber

1 apple

a sprinkle of chia seeds

Note: *After juicing the ingredients, add the chia seeds to your glass. Consume immediately to preserve the seed's crunchy texture.*

Eggplant Greens

Experts say that the darker the color of the vegetable, the more antioxidants it has. The deep purple color of the eggplant's skin is no exception – it contains antioxidants anthocyanin and nasunin which are known to effectively protect the body from cellular damage.

I love this juice recipe not only because it has a thick, delicious taste but all the ingredients combined produce a juice that helps lower the body's cholesterol levels, improves blood flow and even lowers the risk of cancer.

Ingredients:

1 medium Eggplant

2 Carrots

1 Celery Stalk

1/4 cup Spinach

1 Apple

Note: *Juice the whole eggplant, including its skin and seeds.*

Green Juice Fiesta

This recipe is another one of my favorites because it really is a fiesta to my taste buds.

It's a combination of vegetables in a spectrum of colors which guarantees to provide you with plenty of vitamins, minerals and other important nutrients.

Each glass is packed with fiber, sodium and protein plus it contains 0 calories. This is another great green juice recipe to concoct when you have a busy day ahead of you.

Ingredients:

1/4 cup Kale

1/4 cup Spinach

1 Carrot

2 Tomatoes

1/2 Lime

1/2 Green Pepper

1/4 cup Water

Note: *Add water and lime to taste.*

Tomato Zing

Feel like drinking something wild and zingy today? Tomato Zing is the perfect choice.

Tomatoes are powerful antioxidants and have anti-inflammatory properties. They are packed full of Vitamins A and C, iron and calcium. Combine that with the nutrients from leafy greens and your body is sure to stay in optimum shape.

Ingredients:

5-6 Red Tomatoes

1 Lemon

4 pcs. Celery Ribs (with leaves)

1 tsp. Cayenne Pepper

a dash of Salt

Note: *After juicing the produce, squeeze lemon into your glass and add a dash of salt.*

Mean and Green

This green juice recipe supports the health of the pancreas.

Our pancreas is responsible for controlling our blood sugar levels and breaking down the food we consume, so it's important that we support its healthy function.

Brussel sprouts are rich in fiber and Vitamin C and have anti-cancer properties. On the other hand, string beans are high in vitamins and minerals and have anti-inflammatory benefits.

This is one green juice recipe that I drink when I feel like I'm coming down with something.

Ingredients:

3 leaves Romaine Lettuce

8-10 pcs. of String Beans

4 Brussel Sprouts

1 Cucumber

1 Tomato

1/2 Lime

Note*: After juicing the ingredients, squeeze the juice of the lime into your juice. If you want to make this drink a little sweeter, you can add a small apple to the recipe.*

The Dandelion Mix

Dandelion greens are extremely nutritious, but rarely used as an ingredient in green juices. I love this leafy green because it is high in calcium, iron, copper, manganese, potassium and many more important minerals. It is also 14% protein and is loaded with antioxidants.

One reason they are not often used in juice recipes is because of their bitter taste. But adding a fruit or two into the recipe can easily mask the taste of this nutrition powerhouse.

Ingredients:

A big handful of Dandelion Greens

2 Carrots

1 Cucumber

1 Apple

1/2 Tangerine

Note*: Peel apple (if it's not organic), tangerine and carrots but leave the skin of the cucumber.*

Daily Juicing Guide for Weight Loss

Now, here is the most important part of our journey.

You can easily pick out one of the many recipes I listed in the previous chapter and make a refreshing, healthy drink. But if you really want to shed off those extra pounds, it's going to take more than a glass or two of green juice.

Like I mentioned in Chapter 4, most people undergo juice fasting for weight loss.

I understand that it can be pretty tough to do a juice fast without knowing where to start, the ideal duration of your first juice fast or how much juice to drink daily – so that's exactly what we're going to talk about in this chapter.

Juice Fasting Program: A Simple Guide for Beginners

Duration

The average duration of juice fasts varies anywhere from 2 days to 2 months. However, I strongly advise that you start small as a beginner. Remember, successfully finishing a short juice fast is way better than breaking a long one.

2-3 days is a good duration to start with when it's your first time. This will give you ample time to "break in" to

115

your new diet and observe how your body reacts to it. I suggest you start on a weekend (from Friday to Sunday or just Saturday and Sunday) to have flexible time. Juice fasting is a lot of work – shopping and preparing ingredients may take some time and it won't be ideal to start on a school/work day.

Energy/Discomfort

Our bodies show certain reactions when a new diet is introduced; and a juice fast is no different. Some people felt super energized, some people felt slightly sick. When I first started juice fasting, I felt a little nauseous and weak but soon enough it wore off and I started feeling more vital.

Whatever discomfort you feel as you begin your juice fast is just your body adjusting to the new diet. Just think about what it can do to your body in the long run. Also, this is another reason why it's ideal to start your first juice fast on a weekend – so that you have free time to care for any possible discomforts that the new diet brings.

Just remember to limit your physical activity and consume plenty of water while fasting.

Routine

Since you will be substituting your regular meals with fruit and vegetable juices during a juice fast, the most important thing is to keep your calories up to avoid hunger and fatigue. This means that you have to drink 9-12 cups of juice daily.

For this, you have to be prepared to go to the grocery every day or every other day since you will need a lot of produce. I suggest that you start with juices that use carrots and apples as base ingredients. They are safe for first-timers (safe on the taste buds and easy on the stomach), give you a good amount of juice and they're budget-friendly, too.

As you get used to apple or carrot-based juices, you can eventually add more and more new fruits and vegetables to your juices.

Lastly, I advise that you mostly drink fruit juices during the first half of the day as they will fuel your energy and provide your body with complex carbohydrates. For the later part of the day, choose partial or full green juices that are less sweet.

Final Recommendations

It is a fact that good health is earned, not given by God. Anything that you do to improve your health and your lifestyle is a gesture that shows appreciation to the gift of life given to us.

Think about this for a minute – aside from the desire to lose weight, I am hoping that you decided to go on a juice fast simply because you know how valuable your health and your life are. Tell me: is there anything more worth working hard for than your health?

I tried juice fasting because I wanted to feel vital and more alive. I wanted the energy to enjoy life – because if you are unhealthy you won't have the energy to do this. But most of all, I wanted to become healthier. I believe that a healthy body is the key to everything else in life.

So that's it, I believe you are now ready to begin your first juice fast. I am honored to be able to share this knowledge with you and I do hope that you allow fruit and vegetables juices to change your life (and health) for the better like it did mine.

Our journey doesn't end here – it is entirely up to you where you want to take this. Good luck and may the force of fruit and vegetable juices be with you!

Notes

Thank you for buying and reading this book. I really hope you will put it to good use and start juicing.

I encourage you to check out my other books as well. I am sure you will find a lot of useful information in them. They can be found on Amazon.com

If you'd like to discover more healthy tips on how to improve your diet and eating habits, head over to

www.HealthyDietDaily.com

or you can connect with me on Facebook at

www.facebook.com/HealthyDietDaily

Thank you!

Other Books by Donna Hardin:

1. Hearty Organic Cookbook: Your Daily Guide to Organic Cooking Using Fresh, Natural & Healthy Foods

2. Detox Diet Foods Demystified: The Science Behind the Best Detox Foods & How to Detox Your Body the Right Way

3. Top 50 Best Kept Secrets about Detox Diets...Exposed

Bibliography

1. "Juicing Therapy" by Bernard Jensen, Ph. D.

2. "Juice Fasting" by Dr. Paavo Airola, PhD, ND

3. "Raw Juice Therapy" by J. Lust. Benedict Lust Publications

4. "The Uses of Juices" by Clinkard, CE. Penguin Global

Made in the USA
Lexington, KY
06 April 2016